FREAK STORM

Matt Pelfrey

BROADWAY PLAY PUBLISHING INC
New York
www.broadwayplaypublishing.com
info@broadwayplaypublishing.com

FREAK STORM
© Copyright 2008 by Matt Pelfrey

Cover image by Tim Twelves
1st printing: August 2008
I S B N: 978-0-88145-389-8

Book design: Marie Donovan
Word processing: Microsoft Word
Typographic controls: Ventura Publisher
Typeface: Palatino
Printed and bound in the U S A

FREAK STORM was developed with the generous support of the A S K Theater Project and Abby Epstein.

The play received its world premiere on 12 October 2002 in a production by the Lodestone Theater Ensemble (Producers: Tim Chiou, Diana Lee Inosanto, Tony Lathann, Nelson Eusabio, and Philip W Chung), co-produced by the Victory Theater (Producers: Tom Ormeny and Maria Gobetti). The cast and creative contributors were:

LYNN . . . . .Esperanza Catubig
ADAM . . . . Michael Ordona
IAN . . . . Chil Kong
GIL . . . . .Ray Chang

Director . . . . Kipp Shiotani
Sound design . . . . Dennis Yen
Set design . . . . Melanie Shannon
Costume design . . . . .Jae Sun
Lighting design . . . . .Isaac Ho

CHARACTERS & SETTING

Adam
Lynn
Ian
Gil
Jana

All in their twenties

Time: Late at night during an intense, violent rain storm

Place: Ian's S U V. *A rainy street. A second floor apartment in Los Feliz, a neighborhood in Los Angeles.*

(Night. Rain lashes down.)

*(*IAN, *behind the wheel of his Ford Explorer, concentrating on the road.)*

*(*GIL, *next to him, frazzled, drinking a beer wrapped in an old T-shirt.)*

GIL: Wanna wake-up now.

IAN: Huh?

GIL: I wanna wake-up.

IAN: What're you talking about?

GIL: It's like some weird nightmare. *(Beat)* You realize that don't you? That this's the kind of shit you're supposed to wake up from? *(Beat)* But I know I'm awake. I know I'm experiencing this first hand. That's what's so fucked up. *(Takes a drink of his beer)* Like the day before, right? The day before it all goes down, my life's one way. There are rational birds in the trees, Mister Sunshine's givin' me a big thumbs up. The world makes sense. My mind on nothin' more sinister than what new albums are coming out. What flicks hit D V D this week. Then, in like, one fuckin' evil moment, everything becomes this dream sequence. A dream sequence in one of those arty European movies where nobody knows what the fuck's happening but it gives you the big time creeps? *(Beat, thinks a moment)* No, no. Here's what it's like: all the sudden, the sound track of my life is goddamn Marilyn Manson. Before, it was like, some mellow stuff. Something poppy. Like Elton

John maybe. But now it's Marilyn Manson. *(Another pull from the beer. Beat)* You're speeding.

(IAN doesn't say anything.)

GIL: I said *you're speeding!*

IAN: And you're babbling like a hysterical girl.

GIL: I'm not hysterical.

IAN: How many beers is that?

GIL: Dude, seriously, slow down.

IAN: I'm in full control.

GIL: Barely see the road.

IAN: I can see it perfectly.

GIL: Dude, the rain—

IAN: I'm an expert driver, so shut up.

GIL: Well, just so you know, just so you keep this little nugget embedded in the back of your mind, I would prefer to not go flying through your windshield.

IAN: You won't unless I throw you through.

GIL: Also, something for you to mull, we do not wanna be pulled over by the cops. Think about that little mess. Think about that can of worms for a sec, huh? Fuckin' psycho highway patrol, pull that shit they do, messing with honest citizens, makes us get outta the car, got some quota he's trying to meet, searches through the back seat, finds the—

IAN: How about not drinking an open beverage of alcohol, okay? For starters?

GIL: Dude, at this point, we're talking strictly medicinal. *(Beat)* 'Sides, any sane human being would be drinking after the shit we been through.

IAN: No, if you were a man, you'd keep your mind clear and just deal with it.

GIL: We all can't be supermen. All can't be like that dude.

IAN: What dude?

GIL: Your fucking idol. That jar-headed freak.

IAN: Who?

GIL: That singer-slash-poet-slash-spoken-word freak. *(Beat)* How come I can't think of his name?

(Pause)

IAN: Chuck the can, grab some shut eye. Gonna make you take the wheel in Ventura. Stop for coffee or something.

GIL: No fucking way. Never sleeping again.

IAN: You need some badly. Look like a crack ghoul. One of those guys who'd swallow their own dad for a hit a'rock.

GIL: Dude, that's... So fucking gross.

IAN: Thing is, you show up lookin' zombified, that may give Adam an idea something's wrong.

GIL: Gimme a break. I've looked like shit my whole life. He won't blink. *(He takes a long moment, drinks from his beer.)* Maybe we're fucking up.

IAN: We're not.

GIL: I'm saying maybe, just possibly, we are. Let's just call his ass, tell him what's going on.

IAN: Now think a sec. Poor fucker's getting married. Stressed, dealing with all these issues, then he gets a call, we spill the beans, and what happens? I'll tell you: He goes to pieces. Gets wigged, just like you are. Maybe he tells Lynn. You see? Then what does she do?

GIL: Hearing it from Adam's better than the other option.

IAN: It's not gonna come to that. 'Cause we're gonna be looking out. Running interference if the situation comes to it. It's not foolproof, but, hey, it's something. It's a concept. A plan of attack.

GIL: I guess.

IAN: We get there. Play it cool. Under no circumstances do we tell him. Bottom line: I'm Adam's best man...

GIL: Right. You're the best man. How can I forget...

IAN: ...keep your shit wired tight and follow my lead.

(They drive in silence for a moment.)

GIL: Feel bad?

IAN: Of course not. Know why?

GIL: Why?

IAN: 'Cause we didn't do anything wrong.

(GIL shifts in his seat, sips at the beer.)

IAN: All this shit's just an attempt to scare us. *(He stares forward into the night.)*

(GIL takes a long drink.)

(Stage slips into darkness.)

11:35 P M

(Darkness)

(Rain)

(She appears in a sliver of yellowish light, like that of a street lamp. A young woman in her twenties.
Drenched.
Long hair matted against her face.

Clothes soaked.
No protection against the onslaught.
She's either smiling, or crying...or both. Hard to tell.
She looks up at something. Holds out her hands.
They're covered in writing. Or are those scars?
Then, just like that, she steps back into the darkness.
Swallowed up.
Like she was never there.)

11:56 P M

(Stage in total darkness. The storm tears into the night.)

(A phone rings.)

(Lights slowly rise on LYNN *and* ADAM. *They've fallen asleep on the couch. He stirs.)*

(The phone continues ringing.)

(ADAM *opens his eyes. He's in a half sleep. He stares forward a moment or two, then realizing the phone is ringing, lurches over and gets it.)*

ADAM: *(Into phone)* Yeah - hello? Ian? *(Beat)* Hello? *(Listens)* Hello. *(Beat)* If you're gonna crank us, at least get a better cell phone. Can barely hear your heavy breathing. Kind of ruins the effect. *(Beat)* Give it a rest, asshole. *(He hangs up the phone, goes to* LYNN.*)* Skeeter.

LYNN: Hmmmm?

ADAM: Hey.

LYNN: ...What?

ADAM: Wake up.

LYNN: He here?

ADAM: Nah. C'mon, take you to bed.

LYNN: I'm okay. I'm fine. *(Beat)* How long we out?

ADAM: Hour or so. I think.

(Pause)

LYNN: Someone call?

ADAM: The breather again. Told 'im to fuck off. *(Pause)*
He should've been here by now.

LYNN: Rain probably slowed him down.

ADAM: Hang that weatherman. Stormy Rains, Dallas
Mountains...whatever the moron calls himself.

LYNN: Johnny Mountain.

ADAM: Hmm?

LYNN: Weather guy. Channel Two. That's his name.

ADAM: We should do it inside.

LYNN: It'll be fine.

ADAM: Not if it's like this.

LYNN: Want a Vicodin? Cause if you're gonna stress—

ADAM: It's just...can things get more fucked right now?

LYNN: We'll have good war stories to tell.

ADAM: Like our tires getting slashed? There's a great
wedding story.

LYNN: Shit happens.

ADAM: And that invitation?

LYNN: You really are jittery. Haven't given that thing
a second thought.

*(ADAM goes to a stack of wedding stuff, finds the invitation.
Reads from it.)*

ADAM: "I'm coming." Nothing else. No return address.
And all in like, little kid's handwriting. Nice.

LYNN: Bet you anything it's my brother doing his very calculated "weird guy" routine again. If he had his shit together enough to even have a phone I'd call him right now and rag on him.

ADAM: Right.

LYNN: Listen. Things'll be okay. Sure, a storm, quake, who knows...something fucked up could happen. If it does, so what? We're going to get married. Even if the ceremony's under ten inches of rain, the catering messes up, as long as we say our vows, that's the only thing that matters to me, okay?

ADAM: Yeah. *(A breath, relaxing...)* Yeah...you're right. *(Beat)* Better get this place ready to be violated.

LYNN: How's my breath?

ADAM: *(Leans in)* Puppyish.

(ADAM *moves for the hallway.* LYNN *by the window, stares out at the rain...)*

ADAM: Where's the sleeping bag? The blue one?

(No response from LYNN.*)*

ADAM: Hon?

(LYNN *puts her face closer to the window, peers out...)*

ADAM: Lynn...

LYNN: There's someone out there.

ADAM: So what? *(Beat)* Why, is it Ian?

LYNN: Don't think so.

ADAM: Then ww...?

LYNN: No hat. No umbrella. He's just standing there. Getting drenched.

(ADAM *joins* LYNN *at the window.)*

ADAM: That's not a guy.

LYNN: You sure?

ADAM: Her hair's just matted down....

LYNN: *(Leans closer)* Shit, you're right....

(Pause, then—)

ADAM: Where's the sleeping bag?

LYNN: Why?

ADAM: To sleep in? Ian?

LYNN: We'll give him sheets.

ADAM: He doesn't need sheets. He's a dude.

LYNN: Hall closet.

(ADAM exits. LYNN looks back out the window. Her expression changes. She presses her face closer to the glass, as if the woman has disappeared. She is trying to see if she can spot her again. He enters with the sleeping bag, throws it on the couch.)

LYNN: She's gone.

ADAM: Good for her.

(LYNN exits down the hall to the bathroom.)

(ADAM goes into the kitchen, gets a beer from the refrigerator.)

(LYNN enters, stands in the hallway brushing her teeth.)

LYNN: So...run this by me again...

ADAM: He was already on the road. I was taken off guard...just couldn't say "Hey, Ian, turn around, you've been driving for hours but 'fuck you'"—

LYNN: I didn't—

ADAM: You're my best man but "go away".

LYNN: Didn't ask you to say— My only point is we've got a lot of work to do. Not like you won't see him at the bachelor party.

ADAM: He wants to help out.

LYNN: That a quote?

(ADAM *shrugs.* LYNN *exits to the bathroom again. He goes to the window, stares outside. She enters.)*

LYNN: Okay, come, inspect me...

(ADAM *smiles, grabs* LYNN. *Smells her breath, gives her a kiss, starts to get carried away.)*

LYNN: Easy...

ADAM: C'mon...

LYNN: Put your dick away hotshot...not that kind of inspection.

(ADAM *grabs* LYNN, *pushes up on her.)*

LYNN: ...Got company coming...

ADAM: I'll make it quick. I promise. Thirty seconds. As a favor to you. Ten if you call me Thor.

LYNN: ...Good Adam, fuck me in front of the window so the neighbors can see...

ADAM: Live a little.

LYNN: ...serious, don't...

ADAM: Come on, this'll do more for me than a Vicodin...

LYNN: ...Adam...Adam...

(ADAM *stops.)*

LYNN: Thank you.

(But ADAM *isn't paying attention to* LYNN. *He's looking out the window.)*

ADAM: She's back. Standing in the middle of the street.

(LYNN *looks.*)

ADAM: See...?

LYNN: Yeah...

ADAM: Poor lady. *(Pause)* Is she...is she staring up here?

LYNN: Can't tell...

(Pause)

ADAM: She is. She's staring up here. I think... *(Beat)* Step back.

LYNN: Looks like she's laughing...

ADAM: Kinda, yeah...

LYNN: Or...

ADAM: What? *(Pause)* Lynn, what?

LYNN: Crying.

(Big crash of thunder. The lights go out.)

LYNN: Lovely.

ADAM: Where's the flashlight?

LYNN: Book case, I think.

ADAM: All right...hold on... *(He finds the flashlight, turns it on.)* Light some candles.

(LYNN light some candles. ADAM goes back to the window.)

LYNN: Still there?

ADAM: No street lamp. Can't see.

(Someone pounds on the front door. LYNN lets out a startled yelp.)

(ADAM goes to the front door. Opens it. Nobody there. He steps into the stairwell. The second he does, hands grab him, pull him into the darkness. Sounds of a struggle...)

LYNN: Adam—?!

(Laughter erupts from the stairwell. IAN *is pushed inside, followed by* ADAM.*)*

ADAM: *(Laughing)* Dick!

IAN: Ha!

ADAM: *(Shoves* IAN, *playing)* ...kinda shit is that?

IAN: Just open the door for anyone?

ADAM: Knew it was you!

IAN: Right, big city like this? Coulda been some psycho, fuckin' meat cleaver— *(Grabs* ADAM*)* Wack! Wack! Wack!

(The lights flicker back on.)

IAN: God speaks.

LYNN: *(A little wave)* Hey, Ian—

IAN: Lynn, baby...

(They hug.)

IAN: Lookin' great.

LYNN: Yeah, right...

IAN: No, you are.

LYNN: I look tired.

IAN: *(Knows it sounds insincere)* True beauty shines through.

LYNN: Listen to this guy.

ADAM: Hitting on my wife?

IAN: Still fair game for a week and a half.

LYNN: You know, he's right.

ADAM: See that engagement ring? That takes her off the market.

LYNN: You guys are talking like I'm just a product.

IAN: Aren't you?

LYNN: Um, let's see... "No."

IAN: But isn't that exactly what the engagement ring is?
A down payment? It has to be X amount of the dude's
paycheck and whatever? I'd go so far as to say the
entire engagement ring scam is actually degrading
to women because it does equate you to something
that can be bought and paid for.

ADAM: Wish you'd brought this up before I laid down
the cash.

IAN: Should be thinking for yourself, pal. I can't always
do your heavy lifting. It's time you became a man.

ADAM: Was about to say how glad I am you made it
safe, now I'm not so sure.

IAN: Shit, almost didn't. *(Re: the storm)* What's going on?

LYNN: We were just saying—it's crazy.

IAN: Fuckin' weather men—

ADAM: —yes, thank you!

IAN: They're inherently evil.

LYNN: Why's that?

IAN: Common knowledge. I mean, Al Roker? Fucker's
always grinning like he just ate some kid. Watch him
closely next time, it's in the eyes. You can't fake that
kind of darkness.

LYNN: I'm a believer.

IAN: But seriously, this rain—almost cashed out
numerous times. Saw some wicked pile-ups. One
guy near Santa Barbara was holding his Thomas
Guide against his face like a bandage.

LYNN: Ughh!

IAN: Shit, yes, he was all screaming and running around the side of the road and his wife was trying to grab him before he got hit— Very nasty.

ADAM: Beer?

IAN: Bring it on.

ADAM: How 'bout food? You okay, or—

IAN: I'm fine—Gil made me stop in Buellton.

LYNN: Gil?

IAN: He's a freak for Taco Bell. Digs those fuckin' Gorditas.

ADAM: Whoa, hold it: Gil's here?

IAN: Uh, yeah. (Off their tone) What's up? Said me and Gil were coming.

ADAM: You never mentioned Gil.

IAN: Sure I did.

ADAM: No...you didn't.

IAN: Whatever. So what? It's fuckin' Gil. Where I go, Gil will eventually follow.

ADAM: No, no, you're right...

LYNN: We were just...

ADAM: ...kinda "off guard" and, whatever.

IAN: Don't sweat it. This is a humanitarian mission. We were kicking back in Morro Bay and thought, why are we here when we could hit the road, help the young couple prepare.

LYNN: Hope you mean it. Got a lot to get done, 'specially before you guys hit Vegas, so—if you're gonna stay here, I *will* put you to work.

IAN: We're at your disposal.

(Knocking at the front door. LYNN *opens up.* GIL *enters, drenched.)*

GIL: Aaaaaa, fucking apocalypse out there, fucking Noah, man!

ADAM: Gil!

GIL: Heya.

LYNN: Hi, Gil.

GIL: Greetings, salutations, n'all that shit.

LYNN: *(His jacket:)* Let me take that.

GIL: All yours. *(Hands* LYNN *his jacket, smoothes his wet hair)* Goddamn, huh?

*(*LYNN *exits into hallway with jacket.* ADAM *and* GIL *hug.)*

GIL: Jesus, man, you working out?

ADAM: A little.

GIL: Fuck, can tell. Hugging you gave me a serious half-chub.

ADAM: I'm flattered.

GIL: The fucking groom. Huh? Crazy shit.

ADAM: Yeah it is.

GIL: First to get married.

ADAM: Nah, Teddy Schlemer—few years back.

GIL: Fuck Teddy. That dick. He don't count. You're the first officially sanctioned friend to take the dive.

IAN: Hey, how about that beer?

ADAM: Oh, right—Gil? Brew?

GIL: Yes, please.

*(*ADAM *goes into the kitchen.* LYNN *enters.)*

LYNN: Hon, getting them drinks?

ADAM: *(From kitchen)* Got it covered.

IAN: Where'd you park?

GIL: Up the block by that church.

LYNN: Not a church, that's a mosque.

GIL: Fuck's a mosque?

ADAM: *(Comes in from kitchen with beers, hands them out)*
...a church for Muslim dudes.

GIL: They wear those funky head things?

LYNN: Well, some, yeah.

IAN: How's the neighborhood?

LYNN: We love it. Got House of Pies down the street,
a good book store. Getting a tad hip for my taste but...

IAN: I mean, like, crime-wise.

ADAM: What're you asking?

IAN: I gotta worry about my ride getting broken into?

ADAM: It'll be fine.

(IAN goes to the window, stares out.)

IAN: Why didn't you park there?

GIL: Where?

IAN: Fuckin' in front.

GIL: No spots.

IAN: C'mere.

(GIL joins IAN at window.)

IAN: What's that?

GIL: Not a space.

IAN: Plenty of room.

GIL: Not even.

IAN: Could fit two cars there.

GIL: But not one S U V.

ADAM: Who cares?

IAN: Re-park.

GIL: Suck me.

IAN: I'm serious.

GIL: So am I. Get on your knees and suck me.

ADAM: Guys—c'mon?

IAN: Park in front.

GIL: *(Now with an edge)* You.

IAN: I did most of the driving.

LYNN: Ian? You got "The Club"?

IAN: Well...it's a "Gorilla Grip" but same dif.

LYNN: That should be okay.

IAN: *(Gives* LYNN *a courtesy nod, then back to* GIL*)*
I'm serious.

*(*IAN *and* GIL *stare at each other for a few beats.* LYNN *and*
ADAM *exchange a quick glance.)*

GIL: Alright, fine! I'll re-park the piece-of-shit! *(He
downs the rest of his beer.)* You're a real prick.

IAN: I gotta be me.

ADAM: Guys're making a big thing outta nothing—
nobody's out tonight in this shit.

LYNN: No...we saw somebody.

ADAM: Well, yeah, but that was like some homeless
lady wandering around...

GIL: When was this?

ADAM: — like earlier.

GIL: Tonight? Like this evening?

ADAM: Yeah.

LYNN: ...when we were waiting for you.

GIL: And it was a woman?

IAN: Gil, stop fucking around and go.

GIL: Adam saw some lady.

IAN: So what? I see ladies all the time. And upside down they all look the same.

(That was supposed to be a joke. Nobody laughs.)

(GIL holds IAN's look for a moment, then exits out front door.)

ADAM: On the road too long or what?

IAN: I guess. *(Beat, then, somewhat forced:)* Nice place.

LYNN: Yup.

IAN: Kinda small.

LYNN: We see it as "intimate".

IAN: *(Covering)* But I dig it.

LYNN: How's, um—Karen, right?

IAN: Courtney.

LYNN: Yeah.

IAN: Poof.

LYNN: Poof?

IAN: She went away.

ADAM: Harsh.

IAN: Not really.

LYNN: Anyone now?

IAN: Naw, I'm between headaches.

LYNN: Listen to you...

IAN: ...What?

LYNN: Mister Bitter...

IAN: Not bitter.

LYNN: You're like the president of the He-Man woman hater club.

IAN: Adam, am I?

ADAM: Hey, leave me outta this.

IAN: I've had many beautiful, spiritual relationships with chicks. Just dealing with them day in and day out can make your fuckin' brain explode...

(Off LYNN's *look.)*

IAN: Kidding. *(To* ADAM, *who's grinning)* What're you laughing at.

ADAM: Nothing, man—nothing. Just fun watching you step in shit.

IAN: You should talk.

ADAM: Hey, I watch where I'm going, don't pull me into it.

LYNN: What do you mean, Adam should talk?

IAN: Just that...

(Off something in ADAM's *expression)*

IAN: ...forget it.

LYNN: No... *(Looks at* ADAM*)* I wanna know what he's talking about. *(To* IAN*)* What? Tell.

IAN: Just funny, okay—when I'm hanging with friends who have girlfriends, I always notice that if I talk the way we talk when they're not around—not always, but more than not, the chick is shocked or surprised. And they always think it's just me, like I'm the asshole friend. But trust me, usually their boyfriend, or in this case, their fiancé, is the worst, nastiest offender.

LYNN: So tell me what he's been hiding—

(GIL *bursts in the front door.*)

GIL: There asshole, it's in front. Happy?

IAN: Fuckin' ecstatic.

LYNN: Want a towel?

GIL: Please.

(LYNN *exits into hall.*)

ADAM: How 'bout something hot?

GIL: How about another brew?

ADAM: You got it. (*He goes into the kitchen.*)

GIL: (*A whisper, keeping an eye on* ADAM) She's here...

IAN: (*Whispering*) Shut up.

GIL: (*Whispering*) He saw her!

IAN: (*Whispering*) We don't know that...

GIL: (*Whispering*) Who else?

IAN: (*Whispering*) Get a grip before you blow the—

GIL: (*Whispering*) Gotta tell him. Tonight.

IAN: (*Whispering*) Shut up!

(ADAM *comes in from kitchen, hands* GIL *his beer.*)

ADAM: (*Picks up on the vibe*) What?

IAN: (*Goes to the window*) Nothing.

ADAM: Still bitching at each other?

GIL: (*Drains half the beer in one pull, wipes his mouth*) Not me, man, it's that prick.

LYNN: (*Enters with towel, throws it to* GIL) Here you go.

GIL: *(Starts to dry his hair)* Too kind.

ADAM: He park okay?

IAN: *(Distant)* Yeah... *(He stares out for a beat or two, finishes his beer, turns away from the window.)* Adam? *(Holds up empty bottle)* A little more love here?

ADAM: Guys're drinking like fishes.

IAN: Just celebrating your holy union.

ADAM: *(Gestures towards refrigerator)* Well *mi casa, es su casa.*

(IAN goes into the kitchen.)

ADAM: Big Gil. What's the story?

GIL: No story.

ADAM: You okay?

GIL: Why?

ADAM: Dunno. Seem...off.

GIL: Sorry.

ADAM: Nothing to be sorry about—just wanna know what's going on with you.

GIL: No you don't.

ADAM: *(A beat, he tries to read him)* The hell's that mean?

GIL: *(Shrugs)* Nothing, man... *(Sips beer)* ...whatever, y'know?

ADAM: So talk.

GIL: Just tense, I guess.

LYNN: *(Joining in, but a little forced)* Welcome to the club.

ADAM: Really...

LYNN: Adam and I've been going at it all week...

GIL: Mmmm.

LYNN: ...nerves, all the plans we're trying to take care of. It's rough.

(IAN *comes in slurping his beer. The phone rings. Everyone looks.*)

LYNN: Great...

IAN: What?

ADAM: Our crank caller again...

LYNN: God, I hate this shit...

IAN: You've been getting calls?

ADAM: Yeah. Past week.

IAN: Can I take it? I'll scare 'em off. I love fucking with these kinds of assholes.

ADAM: *(Shrugs, looks at* LYNN*)* Go for it. I've tried, but knock yourself out.

(IAN *answers the phone.*)

IAN: *(Into phone)* Hello? *(No answer)* Hello? *(Nods, indicating it's the crank caller)* Listen up. Stop calling here. It's time to back off...got me? *(Beat)* If you can hear me: I... Will... Fucking... Kill...You. I will step on your neck until it breaks.

(IAN *hangs up.* ADAM *gives him a look.*)

IAN: Gotta be firm with these punks.

LYNN: Crank calls creep me out. Always have.

IAN: Probably some naked fifteen-year old whacking off.

(*A long, awkward pause. The energy and conversation stall. Thunder booms in the night.*)

ADAM: This fucking storm.

LYNN: Yeah.

(GIL *just sits there, not making eye contact with anyone.*)

(*A book on the coffee table catches* IAN's *eye. He picks it up.*)

IAN: I dig on this Buddhist shit.

LYNN: Right.

IAN: I'm hurt.

LYNN: What—you don't seem like the introspective type.

IAN: I spent most of my high school years on an intense, personal odyssey. I've delved into many a religious text.

ADAM: Tell her what you used to call it.

IAN: Call what?

ADAM: Your term for all that stuff.

IAN: Losing me here, big guy.

ADAM: She'll think it's funny.

IAN: Dude, no.

LYNN: What? Come off it...tell..

IAN: (*A sharp look at* ADAM) Forget it.

LYNN: Now I gotta know.

ADAM: Tell her. Lynn can handle a peek into the male mind swamp.

IAN: Well, I'm not saying shit.

GIL: Bitch bait. (*Pause. Everyone looks at* GIL) Anything that can be used to impress chicks, whatever it may be, we used to call "bitch bait". Playing guitar, for example, is quality bitch bait. Anything that can give you an edge. Anything that will make a chick believe you're worth boning.

LYNN: I see.

IAN: And let me just add, in my defense, that I did not coin that phrase.

(IAN points at ADAM.)

ADAM: —Uh-uh, wasn't me man—you! All you!

IAN: Nope.

LYNN: Gil?

GIL: *(To LYNN)* It was Adam. *(He helps himself to another brew.)* Anyone for another?

ADAM: Me when I get back. *(He exits down hall to bathroom.)*

(GIL drifts over to the window, tries not to be obvious about staring out.)

(An awkward moment as LYNN and IAN look at each other. They both talk at the same time—)

IAN: *(Over LYNN)* I bet this planning is—

LYNN: *(Over IAN)* So tell me about the girl thing—

IAN: Go ahead...

LYNN: No, you...

IAN: Forget it. Please.

LYNN: Just gonna ask about high school...you guys together...

IAN: What d'you mean?

LYNN: In the old days. You guys date a lot?

IAN: Haven't you kids been over this kind of stuff?

LYNN: Sure, but...just curious about the pre-me Adam.

IAN: Why?

LYNN: Why wouldn't I?

IAN: What's the difference? What's here is what you got.

LYNN: Okay, you wanna know? It's the whole parent thing. Most of the time, you've got brothers and sisters and a mom or dad...they give you a window into who your partner is—baby pictures, stories...and of course, obviously with Adam—I mean, in a way, you guys are all there is. Like the fossil record of his evolution...

IAN: Uh, not sure how to take that—

LYNN: No, no, I'm just—

IAN: Like what, I'm Cro-Magnon and Gil's the missing link?

GIL: Hey: fuck that. I get to be Cro-Magnon, you be the fucking missing link!

ADAM: *(Enters, goes for the beer)* Remind me to get them guest towels.

IAN: Good point. Don't wanna dry my hands on anything that's touched his balls.

GIL: *(Gestures down the hall)* Snake pit?

ADAM: *(Opens beer, takes a drink)* Second door.

(GIL exits. ADAM waits until he's gone, then looks at IAN.)

ADAM: What's with him?

IAN: Who the fuck knows? Been acting like a bitch all day.

LYNN: Hey, you know, Ian...?

IAN: Yeah?

LYNN: Can you do me a huge favor while you're here?

IAN: Love to.

LYNN: Please don't refer to women as "bitches".

IAN: I mean bitch in the universal sense—

LYNN: I don't like it in any sense.

IAN: —don't forget, you are marrying the man who coined "bitch bait" so let's not get too high and mighty.

LYNN: Whatever—just—

IAN: Gil said bitch too—

LYNN: I don't like it. No matter who says it. Okay?

IAN: It's cool. Your house, your rules, right?

(LYNN *sips at her beer. Another awkward beat, which* ADAM *is quick to try and fill:*)

ADAM: How's the store? What's new with the Surf Rat?

IAN: Same old thing. We sodomize the tourists during the summer, rest of the time we get by on the custom board work. We'll see how that goes.

ADAM: So life is good, yeah?

IAN: Is what it is.

(GIL *enters, finds a place to sit.*)

(A lull)

LYNN: Got yourself a girl right now, Gil? Significant other?

GIL: Why?

IAN: She's being polite by faking an interest in you.

LYNN: Hey, it's cool, he doesn't have to—it's okay...

GIL: Actually, I am kinda in a relationship right now.

ADAM: Really?

GIL: Really.

ADAM: Why you holding out on me?

IAN: Blow up girls don't count.

LYNN: Har, har...

ADAM: What's her name?

IAN: Maiden China.

ADAM: No, c'mon...

GIL: You know her. She's actually an old friend from high school.

LYNN: Really? You rekindling a long lost love?

GIL: More that she's hung up on me.

LYNN: Ohhh, an obsessed fan? Gil's got the mojo.

IAN: Gil, maybe you should put your mojo away for now...

GIL: *(After a look at* IAN, *back to* LYNN*)* I'm trying to get rid of her.

LYNN: Why?

GIL: She's acting really crazy. Might be insane... like clinically. She's a cutter.

IAN: Gil, how many times do I gotta tell you to just move on and not give that sick bitch another thought...

LYNN: *(Stands up)* Yes, well, I'm about ready to go to bed.

IAN: *(Looks over at* LYNN*)* Oh, shit, I said "bitch" again... sorry...

*(*IAN *laughs, trying to make light of it, then off* ADAM's *look—)*

IAN: It slipped.

LYNN: Right.

ADAM: I'll be in—just give me a few.

LYNN: Stay up as long as you want. *(She exits down hall to bedroom.*

IAN: Oops.

ADAM: What the fuck, guy?

IAN: Sorry — fucking Gil with his bullshit...

ADAM: Gotta watch that crap around Lynn.

IAN: Did I totally piss her off or what?

ADAM: No, she'll be fine...just tired...don't sweat it. *(To GIL)* Not serious, are you? About the chick? Stalking?

GIL: Ask Ian.

ADAM: I'm asking you.

GIL: Well *ask Ian.*

ADAM: Jesus, man, what is with you?

IAN: Ignore him. He's your classic angry drunk. *(To GIL)* Just like daddy, huh? *(To ADAM)* Check this out. Got something for ya. *(He goes to his pack.)*

ADAM: Bring it on.

IAN: Don't get too excited. Just your wedding gift.

ADAM: Ah.

IAN: Which basically means it's a gift for Lynn, right?

ADAM: That's the sad truth.

(IAN pulls out a wrapped box and hands it to ADAM.)

ADAM: Thanks, man.

IAN: Don't bother opening, it's a cheese board.

ADAM: Fun.

IAN: Just looked at the registry thing and picked it up.

ADAM: Right, that fucking registry. Try to get out of it when you get hitched. Stuff sucks. Gotta walk around the fucking store with this marker-gun-thing and... you don't want a piece of that.

IAN: I have no plans to get even remotely near the wedding beast. And if I ever do, she's in charge of everything.

ADAM: Won't happen that way, believe me.

IAN: Hey, if she wants to get married, she can do all that organization crap. Just tell me when to show up.

ADAM: Talk all you want. If it happens, you're gonna be jumping through the same hoops I am.

IAN: Never.

ADAM: Just wait. *(He makes a slight gesture with the gift, indicating "thanks again", then sets the package aside.)*

IAN: Kinda depressing...

ADAM: What?

IAN: That our friendship has degenerated to me seeing you once every blue moon and giving you a fucking cheese board as a wedding gift.

ADAM: Hey, you know, it's how things work.

IAN: Things?

ADAM: Life n'shit.

IAN: How you figure?

ADAM: I dunno. *(Shrugs)* Forget about it.

GIL: I can sleep in the car tonight.

ADAM: What're you talking about now?

GIL: I don't need to be in the way.

ADAM: Don't be an idiot.

GIL: That way I can make sure nobody breaks into your ride. Plus, you guys probably wanna talk.

ADAM: What would we talk about you couldn't be a part of?

GIL: Fuck I know. Whatever a groom and his best man talk about.

ADAM: That's your problem?

GIL: What?

ADAM: You're pissed off you're not the best man?
I had to pick someone.

IAN: Hey, thanks a lot.

ADAM: No—I just mean—

GIL: The whole tradition's bullshit.

IAN: You're really going outta your way to irk me.

GIL: It's all about you, isn't it Ian?

IAN: Told you not to start with this shit.

ADAM: Hey, you're all my best men. Okay? You, Bax,
Rob.

GIL: But see, that's just it, we're not all your best man.
Only one of us is. What the fuck am I? Huh? What is
this best man shit, anyway? Just a conspiracy to turn
friends against friend so you can move on with your
marriage.

IAN: Let me just go on the record here, to you Gil,
in saying that I am the best man because I am clearly
"the best man".

GIL: Fuck you, you're nothing.

IAN: I should kill you for that.

GIL: You always say that! "I should kill you for that"!
Since we were thirteen!

IAN: Well it's true. I should kill you for that. I won't,
but I should.

ADAM: Guys, can we not get into this right now?

IAN: Yeah, shut your fucking pie-hole.

ADAM: You both have to mellow! Alright?

(ADAM *stares at them both, shakes his head. There's a long
silence.*)

IAN: So. How you know she's the one?

ADAM: Just do.

IAN: Not good enough.

ADAM: How you mean?

IAN: That answer is unsatisfactory.

ADAM: Well, what do you want?

IAN: A response that isn't the surface, co-worker answer. That bullshit is what you tell the weasel in the next cubical. I'll ask you again: How do you know dear, sweet Lynn is Ms Right?

ADAM: I love her.

IAN: Snore!

ADAM: I do, man. That's the answer.

IAN: I'm not disputing you're in love. But you've been in love before. Erica? You wasted four years of your life obsessing over that twisted hag. What's different about Lynn?

ADAM: What do you want, some kind of Hallmark schlock? I just know—she does it for me, uh...she's "it".

IAN: You're about to commit to a chick for the rest of your life and that's all you can say? She's "it"?

ADAM: She answers questions about...being with her I mean—when I'm with her I see my future, y'know? Or how I'd like it to be...like kids? I can totally see myself being a dad now.

GIL: Me too.

(ADAM *gives* GIL *a nod, not really sure what* GIL *is trying to say with that.*)

IAN: So all that tells me is maybe your breeding gene is kicking in. You're in the mood to squirt out some pups. But why Lynn? Why not some other hottie?

ADAM: Don't wanna be with anyone else.

IAN: You have no desire to fuck another chick? Get some courtesy hummer on the first date? Bust a nut with some Betty you never saw before?

ADAM: No.

IAN: Wow.

(GIL *drains about half his beer in one pull.*)

GIL: This really what we want to talk about here?

IAN: It's what I want to talk about.

GIL: Well why don't we talk about something else?

IAN: Don't piss me off.

ADAM: Maybe we should all just grab Zs. Yeah? Guys could probably use it. I know I could.

(Nobody says anything.)

ADAM: That cool?

IAN: Sure. Whatever.

ADAM: Been up since five-thirty.

IAN: No problem man, do what you need to do.

ADAM: Extra pillows and sheets in the hall closet if you need 'em.

IAN: Thanks.

ADAM: Tomorrow. We'll grab Lynn, get some morning grub down the street, discuss global politics.

IAN: I dig it.

ADAM: Gil?

GIL: Cool.

(They all stand. ADAM *hugs* GIL, *then* IAN. *He exits down hallway.* IAN *waits until he hears the bedroom door close, then turns to* GIL.*)*

IAN: Dumbshit.

GIL: Fuck off.

IAN: What was that third degree 'bout someone outside?

GIL: How we know it's not her?

IAN: This is a big city. A big, uniquely fucked-up city. People walk around, yes, even in the rain.

GIL: Either way, sooner or later...we can't be here twenty-four seven. The plan is fucking ill-conceived, dude! And those phone calls...it's her! It's her M O!

IAN: I need you to act like a man with working testicles for once in your life. Can you do that? Can you meet me half way here?

*(*GIL *just stares at him.)*

IAN: That was a direct question requiring a fucking response. Can you handle that?

GIL: Who handled it for us? I didn't have a best man to run interference for me. Just got this shit thrown right in my face.

IAN: I'll go. Take a look around the block. Make sure she's not lurking. Then I'll chill in the car, watch the house. Prepare to intercept if necessary. Okay? We'll trade off. Got me?

GIL: Sure. Whatever.

*(*IAN *waits for a moment, then exits out the front door.* GIL *moves to the window, stares out as lights fade.)*

1:09 A M

(A light from an outside street lamp illuminates the room slightly. The rain has stopped for now.)

(LYNN enters from the hallway, quietly moves through the living room to the kitchen.)

(LYNN opens the refrigerator, pours herself a glass of orange juice. As she shuts the refrigerator, a voice speaks to her from the darkness:)

GIL: Got any more a' that?

LYNN: Geeze, startled me...

GIL: Sorry.

LYNN: No, it's alright.

GIL: Watcha' got there?

LYNN: O J.

GIL: Mind if I steal a glass?

LYNN: Help yourself.

GIL: Muchas gracias.

(GIL walks into the kitchen, pours some juice. LYNN sits at a small table.)

GIL: Pretty goddamn exciting, huh? This whole marriage thing?

LYNN: That it is.

GIL: The big jump.

LYNN: Gotta take it sometime.

GIL: A generation slouches towards adulthood.

LYNN: Mmm.

GIL: Been engaged before?

LYNN: W'kind of question is that?

GIL: Just met a lot of girls, been engaged two, three times. It's like a "thing".

LYNN: This is my first.

GIL: Good to know, good to know. None of that old school Liz Taylor crap.

LYNN: Excuse me?

GIL: Liz Taylor was married, what, eight times?

LYNN: Something like that.

GIL: How could her friends ever attend those weddings without breaking out in laughter?

LYNN: I think two marriages is the absolute max.

GIL: Why?

LYNN: That allows you one screw-up. If the second goes up in flames, it's like, marriage isn't for you.

GIL: Know who I think stays together?

LYNN: Tell.

GIL: Couples from the old days. You know, from that era when you married the first person you slept with. Those worked way better. People should marry who they lose their virginity to. Now, there's way too much time to sample the product.

LYNN: One way to put it.

GIL: You live with someone, have sex, do that whole thing, break up, do it again, someone else...after a while it's ingrained to not be forever.

LYNN: Adam and I'll make it. *(She smiles, looks at* GIL, *waits for him to do the social thing and agree.)*

*(*GIL *doesn't.)*

(They both sip their juice in silence.)

LYNN: Well. Anyway. *(She gets up, goes to the sink, washes out her cup.)*

GIL: He ever tell you how we lost our virginity?

LYNN: Excuse me?

GIL: Did Adam...the two of you ever talked about how, like, we lost our virginity?

LYNN: "We"?

GIL: Yuhuh.

LYNN: "We" as in...

GIL: Me, Ian and Adam.

(LYNN gives GIL an odd look, then smirks, almost laughing.)

GIL: What?

LYNN: Just sounded funny.

GIL: What did?

LYNN: No, sorry— Just got such a serious look in your eyes, like I'm waiting for this bombshell of, I don't know, you guys all had some freaky homosexual experience together in high school.

GIL: Shut up!

LYNN: Hey—you tell me this "we lost our virginity together"—

GIL: Sick!

LYNN: I'm sorry—

GIL: What's wrong with you?

LYNN: Fine, okay, keep it down—people are asleep.

GIL: Whatever...

(Pause)

GIL: Was with the same chick. What I was saying.
He tell you that?

(LYNN's *about to say something when there's a sound at the*
front door. She looks.)

(IAN *enters from outside, stops the second he sees* GIL *and*
LYNN.)

IAN: Hey.

LYNN: What're you doing?

IAN: What's goin' on?

LYNN: Why're you outside?

IAN: Lookin' for something in the car. What's up?

GIL: Having a little chat.

IAN: No shit? About what?

GIL: No big.

IAN: Don't leave me outta things.

LYNN: Gil's telling how you all lost your virginity.

IAN: Well, whatever he said, he's lying. Gil's still a
virgin.

GIL: Yeah, right.

IAN: He gets drunk, shit starts to flow. Right dumbshit?

LYNN: Why do you talk to him like that?

IAN: Like what?

LYNN: Just so fucking harsh all the time.

IAN: Gil doesn't mind. Do you fag?

GIL: Fuck off.

IAN: See, it's all the same to him.

LYNN: To me it's not.

IAN: What'm I supposed to do with that info?

LYNN: Be cool to people when you're in my house. Guys are supposed to be best friends.

IAN: Sure, let's all float on butterscotch clouds.

LYNN: Just don't be a dick.

IAN: Because you don't understand the complex rituals I have with my long time friends, doesn't mean I'm a dick. Just means you're on the outside looking in.

LYNN: I don't need to understand to know when someone's acting like an asshole.

IAN: I get the feeling you have a problem with me.

LYNN: It's late. That's what I have a problem with.

IAN: He's still one of us.

LYNN: What?

IAN: Don't know how he acts with you or your new friends...Don't know what part of him you think you know...but...me and Gil are a part of him.

LYNN: Your point?

IAN: Just see the way you look at us. Like Adam is so much different. But he's not. He is us. We raised him. We're in his D N A.

LYNN: Right.

IAN: I'm fucking serious. When his parents died, who was there? You? No. Me and Gil. We know who he really is.

LYNN: And I don't?

IAN: Not like we do.

LYNN: This isn't a competition. We all love Adam. That's what matters. *(Beat)* And Gil? F Y I? I know how Adam lost his...and I don't see why it matters.

GIL: Then you don't know what happened.

IAN: I'm this close to stretching you right here.

GIL: And I'm starting to not fucking care. Wanna throw, let's throw!

LYNN: Hey— Hey!

IAN: Push me and push me, I'm gonna slap you down.

LYNN: Okay, guys...

(IAN *gets in* GIL's *face.* GIL *shoves* IAN *back.* IAN *grabs* GIL's *arm.* GIL *yanks it back and almost falls on his ass.*)

GIL: Fuck you, Ian!

LYNN: Stop! What's wrong with you? Hey! I do not need this shit!

(IAN *takes a deep breath.*)

IAN: You're right. You are...

(GIL *doesn't say anything else, just moves off into a dark corner near the window.*)

IAN: You're totally right. I'm...like you said, it's late.

LYNN: I'm going to bed.

IAN: Yeah.

LYNN: You guys...please do the same.

(LYNN *exits.* IAN *looks over at* GIL.)

GIL: Don't come near me.

IAN: The fuck was that about?

GIL: She came out for juice.

(*Pause*)

IAN: Get out there.

GIL: You see her?

IAN: If I had, don't you think I'd say? Go.

GIL: My turn to keep the kids company? Can't have them getting scared out there, can we?

IAN: Don't call 'em that.

GIL: What? Kids?

(IAN *nods.*)

GIL: Why not?

IAN: Just don't.

GIL: Got a better idea? Or have you already named yours? That's cool. I'll just go out there then, keep Little Gil and Ian Junior company. That better?

(*A moment passes between them. Finally,* GIL *grabs his jacket and exits out the front door.*)

(IAN *stands there. For the first time, we see something pass over his face. The harsh bravado is replaced by something new: Fear. Dread*)

(IAN *takes a deep breath. He holds out his hands...they're shaking. He makes them into fists as lights slowly fade.*)

2:26 A M

(IAN *by the window staring out into the rain.*)

(ADAM *enters from the hallway. He watches* IAN *a moment before speaking.*)

ADAM: Hey.

(IAN *turns, slightly startled.*)

ADAM: Easy.

IAN: Shit.

ADAM: Jumpy?

IAN: Didn't hear you.

ADAM: How come you're not crashin'?

IAN: Not sleepy.

(ADAM *drifts into the room.*)

ADAM: So...everything okay?

IAN: Sure. I dunno. With what?

ADAM: Stuff. Everything.

IAN: Probably not.

ADAM: What's that mean?

IAN: When's everything okay? Probably not. Why?
How you feelin'?

ADAM: Stress out the ass.

IAN: Yeah.

ADAM: Just, this whole thing...

IAN: Hey, I believe it. Shoulda fuckin' eloped.

ADAM: Not even a possibility.

IAN: Guess you're right. She'd make you pay somehow.
Don't wanna taint things from the beginning.

ADAM: Right...

IAN: Shit like that'll happen in its own time.

ADAM: Thanks.

IAN: Natural order.

ADAM: Hope not.

IAN: No question though, this marriage thing, mentally,
a lot to deal with. No more parties. No more dating.
(*Beat*) My dad used to say getting married's like reading
the same book over and over for the rest of your life.

(*Pause*)

ADAM: What the fuck is going on with you two?

IAN: Nothing.

ADAM: Don't tell me that...

IAN: Dude, don't worry about it. Okay? Everything's cool. Go snooze.

ADAM: How'm I supposed to do that when you and Gil are out here acting like dumb-shits? Fighting in front of Lynn?

IAN: That what she said? We didn't fight. Gil was just being sassy and I had to slap him down, ghetto-style.

ADAM: Why're you guys doing this to me?

IAN: We're not, man, we're not.

(Pause. ADAM sits.)

ADAM: You know, I fucked up on my proposal.

IAN: Fucked up how?

ADAM: Was just lame. Had everything set. There's this kick-ass bridge with all these great lamps on your way to Pasadena...I was gonna propose to her on it.

IAN: And you didn't?

ADAM: No. Asked her to marry me while she was taking the fucking garbage out.

IAN: Are you brain-dead?

ADAM: Was like momentary insanity. Just blurted it out. Don't know why. I mean, it was cool and all, she was happy, but there was just...there was just this sense of profound...lameness.

IAN: So she's put the pressure on to deliver a perfect wedding or something?

ADAM: Not at all. Hasn't said anything like that. I just feel it. Just feel like, if we don't start this journey off right...it's like bad luck. Or a curse...or...I don't wanna go overboard, but...I gotta do this right, man. I gotta pull this off. Know what I'm saying?

IAN: Yes. And you will. Me and Gil, we're here to make it happen.

ADAM: Yeah, yeah, I know.

IAN: What?

ADAM: Look...You guys can't be here fucking around.

IAN: We're not. We won't.

ADAM: Ian, listen. I appreciate you showing up and, and—but this isn't going to work with you both staying here. It's a totally cool gesture, but...we should just stick with the plan and meet in Vegas.

IAN: This is Lynn talking, isn't it? She told you to kick us out?

ADAM: No, Ian, it's me. This is coming from me and it's not "kicking you out" either...wait, where is Gil?

IAN: Outside. Getting some air.

(ADAM *reads* IAN's *face. Doesn't buy it*)

ADAM: This is exactly what I'm fucking talking about. I don't need this shit. Tomorrow, you guys clear out. I'm sorry.

(*A moment.* IAN *makes a decision. He goes to the light switch near the front door, flicks the outside light on and off.*)

ADAM: What's this, your secret code?

(*Beat*)

IAN: The bachelor party's not gonna happen.

ADAM: Dude, you're taking this the wrong way. It's just we need space before—

IAN: Not because of this.

ADAM: Then what the fuck?

(Beat)

IAN: Kitzman.

ADAM: Who?

IAN: Jana Kitzman.

ADAM: So?

IAN: She's back.

ADAM: Good for her.

IAN: And pissed.

ADAM: About what?

IAN: That night.

ADAM: Yeah, right.

IAN: Serious.

ADAM: Fuck off, Ian.

IAN: No, Adam, listen: she's very, very upset.

ADAM: What does this have to do with my bachelor party?

(GIL enters from outside.)

ADAM: You guys, so help me, you better start spilling your guts right fucking now.

IAN: Tell him.

GIL: What're you doing?

IAN: Gil, this is what you wanted, right? With your little fucking hints and shit to Lynn.

GIL: I thought—

IAN: Plan's changed.

ADAM: He says Kitzman's back in town.

GIL: Uh-huh.

IAN: Tell him Gil.

(Pause)

IAN: Tell him.

(Pause)

GIL: Three days ago. I'm working, swiping groceries, ten items or less, look up to ask for a price check and there she is. *(Beat)* Jana Kitzman. *(Beat)* Staring right at me. *(Beat)* Jana. Fucking. Kitzman. 'Sept she doesn't look like she did. I mean...time hasn't been good to her. Got all these weird fuckin' tats on her arms. Her face. Piercings. Scars.

ADAM: You fucking liars.

IAN: Not lying.

GIL: Asked me to meet her at Morro Rock.

ADAM: You guys, both of you, bullshit junkies. I'm not taking the bait. Kitzman did not show up and whatever else.

GIL: So I go out to the Rock after work. Fog was in. Pitch black out there. I'm nursing a King Cobra, listening to the waves explode against the breakers. And then, she just like, materialized at my window.

(Pause)

ADAM: What did she want?

GIL: What do you think?

ADAM: Well, seeing as the last time I saw her was in high school, I can't say I know.

GIL: ...that night...at the ashtray.

ADAM: Yeah? And? *(Reads GIL's face)* That was nothing. She started all of that. *(Beat)* 'Sides, she wasn't angry then, was she?

GIL: Well...she is now.

ADAM: And...so...?

(Silence)

IAN: She says...that night...she got pregnant.

ADAM: Fuck you.

IAN: That's not all.

GIL: She had triplets.

IAN: And you, me and Gil are the daddies.

GIL: That's what she said. One for each of us.

ADAM: You guys really think I'm gonna fall for this shit?

IAN: She's coming here. You're next on the list.

ADAM: Oh, well, if she's coming here, let's keep the door open for her. *(He crosses, opens the door, leaves it wide.)*

GIL: Fuck, don't—! *(He rushes over and shuts it.)*

ADAM: See, Lynn doesn't understand, but this is why I love you guys. Seriously. Unprecedented. And pulling Kitzman out of the air like this...kind of fucked up, but... Great joke.

IAN: *(To GIL)* Bring 'em in.

GIL: You sure?

IAN: Yes, I'm fucking sure.

ADAM: Bring what?

GIL: The kids.

ADAM: Okay, I guess I should let you play this out. Go ahead, bring the kids in.

IAN: Hurry up.

(GIL exits out front door.)

ADAM: So which of you thought this shit up?

(IAN *stares at* ADAM *a long beat.* ADAM *sees the fear in his friend's eyes. It's starting to sink in.*)

IAN: Dude, you gotta listen to me. This is not a fucking prank.

ADAM: I'm supposed to believe Kitzman showed up...

IAN: Yeah.

ADAM: And said all that?

IAN: Yep.

ADAM: I'm sorry. I don't.

IAN: You will.

ADAM: If this was true...you would've called me the second this shit went down and told me...

IAN: Yeah, of course. "Hi Adam. Hope the wedding stuff is going well. By the way, there's a psychotic hose-beast from your past stalking you. Don't get nervous saying your vows." Come on.

(*Silence*)

ADAM: Explain this shit to me. I mean, what's your recollection of her? Am I completely wrong? She wasn't pissed...

IAN: Not that I remember. Never had classes with her. But hey, that was a kinky night, I don't know... afterwards, maybe she starts to feel weird about what she did, can't reconcile her actions—decides nothing is her fault, typical Oprah shit.

ADAM: Tell me about these kids.

IAN: Brotha, words can't describe it.

ADAM: Did she hear about my wedding?

IAN: Maybe.

ADAM: She dangerous? Think she'd do something to me? Or Lynn?

IAN: Anything's possible.

(The handle of the front door turns. IAN and ADAM, jumpy, look over. GIL enters with a duffle bag.)

GIL: Where?

IAN: Table. And lock that.

(GIL locks the door, then sets the duffle bag down on the coffee table. ADAM and IAN gather around. GIL takes out two jars full of murky red liquid. In each jar is a shape. They have arms. Legs. Little heads)

ADAM: Holy shit...

(The storm intensifies The lights flicker a bit, but stay on.)

IAN: Bottom line, that was a wild, horny night. But hey, you get drunk and fuck a bunch of guys, that ain't rape. It just means you got drunk and fucked a bunch of guys.

ADAM: That's what she's saying?

IAN: Yep.

ADAM: That we assaulted her?

IAN: Yeah, Adam, yeah. She thinks we jumped her bones and put three buns in her oven.

ADAM: *(Picks up the jar)* And this?

IAN: Could be anything. She had some kind of miscarriage, who knows who's kids these are. Who the fuck would save something like this? I mean, case closed. Hell, might've even bought these, some science thing...barely look human. Probably not even real.

ADAM: But why? I don't get...I mean, if she really got pregnant, why not say something at the time?

IAN: Wanna know my personal theory? My sister.
Kept getting fired from jobs—

ADAM: I don't wanna talk about your sister, I want—

IAN: Just listen. It's relevant. She couldn't keep a
relationship. Two divorces, finally goes into therapy,
they do some shit, regression stuff, now she's got all
these memories of a baby-sitter taking her into a yellow
room and screaming when she's like, four years old or
something, and that's why she's a total fuck up. Insane
stuff. Probably the same crap. Kitzman leaves, moves,
whatever happened to her, maybe she gets pregnant by
some toothless auto mechanic or something...but her
life isn't what she wants it to be, can't figure out why
things aren't like T V, and she latches onto this night as,
like, the reason things suck. Fuck that, I'm not gonna be
her bad guy.

GIL: How d'you know we aren't?

IAN: Cause I was fuckin' there.

ADAM: Barely.

IAN: Meaning what?

ADAM: Like you said, we were all smashed!

IAN: Exactly. If she's drunk and you're drunk,
it's just two drunks boning.

ADAM: Jesus...

IAN: You actually entertaining the idea we did
something wrong? We didn't. Get over it.

(*A moment. IAN tries to read ADAM's face.*)

ADAM: I'm fucked.

IAN: You're not—

ADAM: You guys gonna be my bodyguards?

IAN: Just until she shows up.

ADAM: Come on, get real!

IAN: You need to check your stones here, man.

ADAM: But this...this...

IAN: Wanna marry Lynn? Huh? You want the wedding to go right?

ADAM: Of course...

IAN: Then suck it up.

GIL: Maybe we're just gonna get what we deserve.

IAN: Which is what? To get haunted and emotionally abused by some sketchy chick we partied with in high school?

(GIL stares at them a moment.)

IAN: What, Gil? *What?* You look like you either need to take a shit or say something. Which is it?

GIL: I remember...waking up the next day with this hangover. Barely remembering what happened. But afraid. Afraid and feeling like...like this bad dream was out there...circling me...and the rest of the weekend, I just stayed in bed. Waiting for...don't know what. Something to come knocking, kick my door down, drag me out of bed...punish me... When I got to school on Monday, I was... was almost frantic...looking for Kitzman, just needed to see...to see her...there...being normal... found her at nutrition break in the cafeteria. She was sitting there with her friends. I walked by and she made eye contact with me. I said "Hey." And she said "Hey." *(Beat)* And that was it.

IAN: Dude, you had sex and felt guilty the next morning, what's that mean? That you're fucking Catholic? *(Beat)* Both of you listen up: I'm gonna drop some shit on you. She claims we all nailed her. *All of us.* Which is why I know her entire trip is fuckin' corrupt.

ADAM: Why?

IAN: I never did it. Okay? There. Boom. I never drilled her.

GIL: Liar!

IAN: To quote the Dead Kennedys, I was "too drunk to fuck".

ADAM: When you came outta the car, you told me you just popped her.

IAN: Bro, I was fuckin' embarrassed! Here's my chance to be a man, and I couldn't get lift off. But the point is, she says I did, but I didn't. Thus, how can anything she's saying about that night be true? It can't. I mean, come on—that whole evening was a blur, but I'd know if I lost my virginity, and I didn't. And after you two pussies got your groove on, I sure as shit wasn't about to amend my story. I sure as hell wasn't gonna go to school on Monday, sit in Boomer's English class with Gil knowing he's more man than me.

GIL: You fucking asshole.

IAN: Don't even, Gil.

GIL: The only reason I did it was I thought you did.

IAN: Stop it. You did it because you're a guy and that's how God made us.

GIL: I don't feel right about this...

IAN: Well tough titties!

ADAM: You think she's here?

GIL: Fuck yeah she is!!! That crank call was her! She did it to me too.

IAN: Gil, please. Acting like a hysterical gynch helps nothing.

(ADAM *looks off, lost in a thought.* IAN *notices.*)

IAN: Talk.

(ADAM *shakes his head.*)

IAN: No, what're you thinking?

(Pause)

ADAM: Lynn.

IAN: What about her?

ADAM: Gotta tell her.

IAN: Wrong.

ADAM: No. I do.

IAN: Why?

ADAM: She has a right to know...

IAN: What, exactly?

ADAM: Who I am.

IAN: And who's that? Hmm? The Night Stalker?
Fuckin' Ted whatever-his-name was?

GIL: Bundy. Mark Harmon played him in the—

ADAM: We're getting married—

IAN: Yes, I know.

ADAM: Do you? I'm not sure you grasp what—

IAN: Tell her everything that's ever happened to you,
she'll still never know you—

ADAM: Bullshit—

IAN: Think we know each other?

ADAM: Yeah, Ian, I do.

IAN: Let me guarantee you something, I have no clue
who I really am. Deep down. In the pit. And if I don't,
how do you? *(Beat)* Gil, who are you?

GIL: Beats me.

IAN: All telling her does is poison the well.

ADAM: You're wrong...

IAN: Look, if you tell her she'll hate you not for what you did, but for the fact you weren't man enough to digest your own poison. You couldn't keep it in.

ADAM: The truth counts for something.

IAN: Actually, it doesn't.

ADAM: What the fuck do you know about dealing with women, huh? Zero! You got the emotional intellect of a sixteen-year-old!

IAN: I'm trying to help you out, dick.

ADAM: Yeah, lie to my wife!

IAN: I'm trying to think clearly while you're about to brown your undies.

GIL: If we didn't do anything, why shouldn't he tell? I mean, if it's like you say, why not?

IAN: 'Cause it's a fucking weird, grey area. You guys are sperm brothers. You both did fuck her within the same hour. That right there is generally considered morally dubious. And trust me, situations like this, the chick is always right. Always. *(Beat)* Look, if you have to tell her anything, tell her I did it.

ADAM: No, no, no—

IAN: Tell her I messed with this chick, but she thinks it was all of us.

ADAM: Fuck that.

IAN: Why not?

ADAM: You just don't get any of this, do you?

IAN: Lynn can hate me. Not like I'm gonna be coming around much anymore.

ADAM: Shut up.

IAN: Hate to say this, but Gil's right.

ADAM: About?

IAN: Same way he's in a funk 'bout not being your best man. This is it for us. Fuck, half of me's surprised you even made me the best man. Gotta have some buds up here—

ADAM: I don't.

IAN: You must.

ADAM: You're wrong.

IAN: You even know what I've been doing the last year or two? *(Beat)* If you want her to know about this, let me do it. Hey, my wedding gift, right?

ADAM: This isn't the end of anything.

IAN: Dude, wife, then kids, then career. All we got is the old days. Let me eat the glass. You tell her...why take the risk?

ADAM: I want her to know me.

IAN: She does. She does you fucking idiot.

(Beat)

GIL: Maybe...maybe we should go out there and find her. Talk to her. Apologize.

IAN: Another shitty idea from the peanut gallery.

ADAM: Wait—we say we're sorry. It might help. If we just, extend our paw in friendship, that might be enough.

IAN: Oh, come on you guys!

GIL: Fuck you, Ian! You don't know! We gotta do somethin'!

IAN: See these jars? This is what her mind looks like. Shriveled and fucked-up scary. In fact, I think these are the problem... *(He grabs one of the jars.)*

ADAM: Ah, what're you doing?

IAN: Taking care of business. *(He goes to the sink.)*

ADAM: Hold on...

IAN: You'll thank me for this... *(He opens the jar, pours out the liquid, puts the fetus-thing in the garbage disposal.)*

ADAM: No...no, no—don't!

(IAN flips the switch. The disposal grinds and grinds until ADAM shoves past IAN and turns it off.)

IAN: Problem solved.

ADAM: Goddammit! That was—aw, fuck, man...

GIL: I'm gonna be sick!

IAN: Buckle up, man.

GIL: ...uh...I'm serious.

IAN: Bring your jar over here. Do what I did.

GIL: No.

IAN: C'mon! It's therapeutic

GIL: No fucking way!

IAN: Fine. Put everything on my shoulders. Nothing new.

(IAN crosses to the remaining jar. GIL steps in front of him.)

GIL: I said no.

IAN: What do you want it for? Gonna put it on a shelf? Sleep with it under your pillow? I got an idea, why not hang it from your rear view mirror!

(IAN shoves past GIL and grabs the jar. GIL shoves IAN back.)

IAN: Don't do that again.

(IAN reaches for the jar. GIL shoves him again. IAN grabs GIL and they fall in a rough, messy melee.)

(ADAM yells at the guys, rushes in to break it up.)

(LYNN enters from the hallway.)

LYNN: Hey hey—what is this?

(They all stop, look at LYNN.)

LYNN: You guys wrestling around like a bunch of assholes—Adam?

ADAM: Honey—we're...nothing. Go back to bed.

IAN: We're just playing—sorry...

ADAM: I'll be in in'a minute...

(Something's weird, and LYNN can sense it. She just stands there, looking at them. ADAM steps between LYNN and the remaining jar on the coffee table.)

ADAM: Honey, please go to bed.

(Pause)

(LYNN looks from ADAM to IAN, to GIL.)

LYNN: *(Re: the jar he's trying to hide)* What's that?

ADAM: It's...it's...

LYNN: Move.

GIL: Aw, man just fuck it!

IAN: Gil...

(ADAM moves aside. LYNN sees the jar.)

LYNN: What the hell...?

IAN: It's nothing...a novelty I bought, a gag wedding present.

(LYNN moves to the jar. Peers inside)

LYNN: Is this? It looks like...what is it?

IAN: Lynn, I—this is my fault—

ADAM: Ian, no. *(Beat)* There's a girl...

GIL: And she's coming here! Been following us around! She's fucking stalking us!

ADAM: Gil, shut the fuck up!

(LYNN still stares at the jar, transfixed by the ghastly sight.)

LYNN: What girl...?

(Pause)

LYNN: Adam? What girl?

ADAM: She's thinks we took advantage of her or something.

LYNN: Wait...

ADAM: Says we messed with her...back in high school.

(Pause)

LYNN: "Messed with her"?

ADAM: Yeah.

(Pause)

LYNN: Messed with her how?

GIL: Raped! Just say it! Raped!

LYNN: What?

IAN: Lynn, Adam didn't do anything wrong...this chick just...she's unhinged. Nothing happened that she didn't start or want.

LYNN: In high school...?

ADAM: Yeah.

(Another long pause as LYNN tries to get her mind around the situation. Still hard to look away from that jar.)

LYNN: Adam? *(Looks at* ADAM*)* Adam, *say something!*

(Pause)

ADAM: Like what? I don't know what you want....

LYNN: What's going on goddamit!? Why would this person think you...? I mean...just...tell me why she thinks...

(Pause)

ADAM: It...started at the ashtray. Uh, just this party and—

LYNN: Wait. The what?

ADAM: This parking lot all the surfers use. Near Morro Bay High. Great view of the swells. Called it the ashtray. We were partying. Hooked up with this chick—

LYNN: Does she have a name?

(Beat)

ADAM: Jana.

LYNN: Use that.

(Beat)

ADAM: We get there—

GIL: No, first her friends split.

ADAM: Right. We dropped two of them off at the Quick Mart. The rest of us went to the 'tray. That's when her and Ian got hot and bothered.

LYNN: She was into this?

IAN: Fuckin' totally. We're leaning against my car, making out, she's got my 501s unbuttoned, her hand in my pants—I actually got embarrassed 'cause I thought she was gonna get freaky right there in front of Gil and Adam. So we got into the car, and she's just fucking on fire.

LYNN: Where are you and Gil?

ADAM: Hangin'.

GIL: By the dunes.

ADAM: Gettin' baked. Then we wandered back. That's when Ian came out of the car, pulling his pants up, said she wanted more.

LYNN: And so you and Gil...?

ADAM: Yeah.

LYNN: One after another?

ADAM: Basically.

(LYNN *stares at* ADAM.)

ADAM: What?

LYNN: What do you think?

IAN: Whatever this nut thinks happened, didn't.

LYNN: *Don't call her a fucking nut!* Just...stop it.

ADAM: Just because we had sex with her doesn't mean something criminal happened. People get crazy. Fuck around. We can be a messed up species at times. That's just a fact.

IAN: He's right. He's totally—

LYNN: Like I don't know that? I've got plenty of friends who have done very "out there" things! But none of my friends, after they did something wild, chased the guys they fucked years later. *(The jar)* And that thing?

ADAM: She said she got pregnant that night. Had triplets. One for each of us—

IAN: Which is impossible.

ADAM: Miscarriages apparently. Saved them. Wants to give us each a little present. They're just a twisted hoax.

IAN: ...She probably lives in a basement, listens to the Cure twenty four hours a day and reads Ann Rice...

GIL: We gotta go out there...

IAN: Yeah, right.

GIL: We do. We have to.

IAN: Sit tight.

(GIL *grabs his jacket.*)

GIL: Get your shit, we gotta go and talk to her!

IAN: Gil—!

GIL: All of us. We can find her, talk, fucking apologize or something...

IAN: We're way past the apology phase. I'd be surprised she doesn't try and stick a knife in your eye!

GIL: I don't care. I'm doing this.

IAN: You're being a fucking idiot.

GIL: So what else is new? (*He exits out the front door.*)

(*Pause*)

ADAM: Ian...

IAN: Yeah?

ADAM: Go with him.

IAN: Pass.

ADAM: I mean it.

IAN: Not gonna go look for her, no way. Gil wants to run around like an idiot, he can.

ADAM: Didn't say you had to. Just...go. I need...me and Lynn...we need...

IAN: Look, you guys have to talk, I understand. I can crash in your room if you want...

LYNN: Ian, please, just get in your truck and go.

IAN: You know, I did just drive all night, I'm not—

LYNN: *I want you out of here!*

IAN: Dude, control your woman.

ADAM: Ian, I'm sorry...

(Pause)

IAN: I don't believe you...

ADAM: Grab a hotel, we'll talk tomorrow. Just, right now, at this minute, Lynn and I...

IAN: Fuck that shit.

ADAM: Hey—

IAN: After all I've been— no, this is bullshit. Total fucking bullshit. *(Beat)* What're you gonna do when this bitch shows up? Huh? When she comes up to your door and knocks. Gonna invite her in for tea and crumpets?

ADAM: Fuck you, Ian.

(IAN grabs his stuff, goes to the door...)

LYNN: *(Re: the jar)* Take that thing with you!

IAN: Keep it. Consider it another wedding present. Sure beats the cheeseboard, huh? *(He exits.)*

(LYNN locks the front door.)

(A long silence)

(Finally, LYNN and ADAM make eye contact.)

LYNN: How come I've never heard about this girl before?

ADAM: Why should I?

LYNN: ...Seems like the kind of thing someone who's supposed to be intimate would know.

ADAM: It wasn't a big deal. At all.

LYNN: What does that say?

ADAM: I suppose I know everything about you?
I know every guy you've fucked?

LYNN: We're not talking sexual histories here. We're
talking whether you assaulted someone.

ADAM: You should have that answer.

LYNN: How?

ADAM: Just should. You about to marry the kind of guy
who'd force himself on a girl too drunk to stop him?

LYNN: I don't think so.

ADAM: Don't sound too sure.

LYNN: I'm not.

ADAM: Thank you very much.

(Silence)

LYNN: If she shows up, what—?

ADAM: No idea.

(Silence. The rain grows in intensity.)

LYNN: Please.

ADAM: What?

LYNN: Tell me.

ADAM: Lynn...

LYNN: Please.

(Silence)

ADAM: After Ian said she wanted more, he kinda
gave me a shove towards the car. And there was this
moment when I was...just gonna say no, right? And,
that's actually what I could swear I did say, in my mind

at least. But, I didn't. Didn't say anything. Just kinda
trotted up, opened the door, crawled into the back seat.
She was laying there. Not making any noise, nothing,
just there...and I was like, "Here we go, this is the big
moment." And I move on top of her, and the first thing,
the first, I don't know—was how she wasn't moving
much. I get on her, and she didn't wrap her arms or
legs around me, nothing. I was...you know, I thought
she—you have to understand how drunk we were—
but I was thinking when Ian told me she wanted the
rest of us, that she was just this crazy nympho, and why
should I argue with that? But I get between her...ah, and
she's just not moving at all...just breathing there, and
I try to focus on her face, but it's hard, everything's soft
and blurry, blood pumping away from my brain, and
her hair, she had kinda long hair, it was over her face.
(His voice starts to shake) And that was like this moment
when...I just stopped and kinda absorbed the scene,
and...and...her flesh wasn't inviting, was clammy,
and the car smelled, musty and thick, sweat mixed
with Speed Stick and whatever perfume she had
been wearing, and stronger, the smell of alcohol,
everywhere, those clove cigarettes we used to smoke...
and then I look back down at her... *(Pause)* ...You've got
to understand what it's like...I mean, before you've ever
had sex...as a guy, I mean, maybe it's the same for you,
but...nothing could possibly be more important than
getting it. Nothing on the planet can possibly equal that
fucking primitive urge...to find out what it's all about
for real...nothing, absolutely nothing seems more
impossible to attain...you have no idea what kind of
power you...all of you...hold over us. *(Beat)* ...Once I
was inside her, she still didn't move, at all...so I pushed
the hair from her face, the slick strands, and—there was
no expression on her...just blank. Don't know if that
was because the booze, or...but she was just staring up
at the...nothing. Her eyes were glassy...moist...and I

swear I almost got off her right then and there, pulled out of her...but...instead...I though to myself..."Nobody will notice" and I just...kept going....

(Pause)

LYNN: Who the fuck are you?

ADAM: I'm sorry.

LYNN: Sorry?

ADAM: What else can I say?

LYNN: Sorry doesn't come near what...what—

ADAM: Lynn...

LYNN: No...I can't...Jesus...gonna be sick...

ADAM: Here. Sit down.

LYNN: Don't touch me!

ADAM: Lynn—

LYNN: No, don't. Don't you touch me...

(Silence)

ADAM: I'm getting you something to drink.

LYNN: I don't want to drink!

ADAM: Well what? What the fuck can I do?

(Pause)

LYNN: I want you...to get out of here.

ADAM: Lynn, what—? I mean, c'mon...

LYNN: I mean it Adam. I want you to go.

ADAM: Where?

LYNN: Away. I can't...can't deal with this.

ADAM: I'm not leaving.

LYNN: Not asking you, Adam. I'm telling.

ADAM: You don't understand—

LYNN: I think I do.

ADAM: She's coming...to confront me, I guess...those crank calls... They're her. *(Beat)* She might hurt you. *(Beat)* She's crazy...

LYNN: No...

ADAM: What...?

LYNN: ...that word...

ADAM: What're you—?

LYNN: Crazy. Don't talk about her that way.

ADAM: She's handing out fetuses in jars, I think it kind of applies.

LYNN: No... She's not the bad guy.... She's not the monster.

(ADAM stares. Then:)

ADAM: I'm a guy who made a mistake.

LYNN: "Mistake"?

ADAM: Yes! That's *exactly* what it was!

LYNN: You ruined a girl's life!

ADAM: I told you! I thought she wanted me...
I just couldn't stop once I realized—

LYNN: Yeah, I heard you the first time.

ADAM: I know I was wrong—

LYNN: Do you?

ADAM: Yes.

LYNN: Do you really get it?

ADAM: Of course.

LYNN: Before you said it wasn't a big deal! *(She stares at him.)* In the morning...

ADAM: In the morning, what?

LYNN: You go.

ADAM: Where?

LYNN: I don't care. *(She looks away.)* I'm going to bed.

ADAM: No.

LYNN: And maybe when I wake up in the morning this will've crawled back into the nightmare world... *(She moves to go back into the bedroom.)*

ADAM: Don't... *(Beat)* Don't walk away. *(He moves to her, grabs her arm.)* How can you throw everything away because one time I made the wrong decision...one time.

LYNN: How do I know this is the only time?

(ADAM takes a step back, as if physically slapped. Blinks. Stunned)

ADAM: I can't believe— You really think that's me? If so, if you think that...I deserve to be defined by five drunk minutes when I was eighteen...and that you've somehow been completely wrong for the last four years—if you truly think I'm some monster beyond any fucking forgiveness or repentance or...fine... If that's what you think, then fuck it. We can go our own way. But I guarantee, whoever you fall in love with down the road—no, forget it.

LYNN: No...what?

ADAM: Everyone...everyone's got something they've done. Good people do bad things...horrible things... all the time. If forgiveness is only for small shit... forgetting an anniversary or some bullshit and not for big things...bad things...then it's fucking meaningless.

(Pause)

LYNN: There is no way...no possible way...the person I love could have done that. No way the person I want to marry, have children with...could do that to another human being. Just no way.

ADAM: Fine then. Fine. If that's your view of the human condition, this black and white stark fucking bullshit, if that's the depth of your—if you can't forgive me, if you—hey, fine. I guess you're not who I thought you were either. Guess we've just been strangers pretending we know each other.

LYNN: I guess so.

(But then, as if losing faith in his own anger, ADAM's tone shifts:)

ADAM: You don't believe that. There's no way you believe that. You know me. You still love me. It can't evaporate this quick.

(LYNN stands there. ADAM breaks.)

ADAM: I'm sorry. I'm so fucking sorry.

(Pause)

LYNN: I'm not the one who can forgive you.

(ADAM goes to the couch.)

ADAM: Come here. Sit with me.

LYNN: Adam...

ADAM: Please... *(Pause)* Please. Just sit. Nothing else.

(LYNN moves to the couch. Tentative. Sits away from ADAM.)

(Neither says a word. Numb. Tired. Drained)

(Outside, the rain intensifies. Pouring down in sheets. Rhythmic now. No longer angry. Mournful. Somehow soothing)

(They stare forward as lights fade.)

4:22 A M

(In darkness, the sound of the storm rises, getting louder, violent, intense...finally, the lights rise to previous levels.)

(As this happens, the intensity of the storm goes down to just heavy rain.)

(ADAM and LYNN have fallen asleep on the couch.)

(The phone rings.)

(LYNN sits up. Groggy. Stares at the phone. It keeps ringing.)

(ADAM stirs.)

(LYNN gets up, moves slowly to the phone.)

(ADAM opens his eyes.)

ADAM: *(Groggy)* ...Don't...

(LYNN answers the phone.)

LYNN: *(After a moment)* Yes...? *(Listens a beat)* What is it you want from us? *(Pause)* We know about the jars, okay, we know—

(LYNN stops abruptly. Listens. ADAM gets up from the couch.)

ADAM: Lynn...?

(Pause)

LYNN: *(To ADAM, a whisper)* She's outside. Right now. She's out there.

(ADAM goes to the window.)

ADAM: Can't see shit...

(A long moment as LYNN listens to Jana talking. Finally—)

LYNN: *(Into phone)* What? No...that's not true...that...no...

ADAM: What's she—Lynn? *(Crosses to her)* Gimme that—

LYNN: *(Pulls away)* She's coming...but...but not to give you a jar...

(ADAM just looks at her.)

(Beat)

LYNN: Yours lived. *(Beat)* Your baby lived. *(Into phone)* Yes, I heard you! *(To ADAM)* You're a father.

ADAM: No fucking way...

LYNN: She's bringing him up. To see you. Now.

ADAM: She's lying.

(LYNN lets the phone drop from her hand.)

ADAM: She's lying, Lynn. She's gotta be—

(They're startled by three slow, deliberate knocks at the front door [two beats between each knock]. They both stare.)

ADAM: Maybe...we can...if we don't...she'll go away.

LYNN: She's not going away. This will never go away.

(Knock)

(Knock)

(Knock)

LYNN: Open the door.

ADAM: No...

LYNN: Adam. Open the door.

ADAM: Hell no...

(Knock)

(Knock)

(Knock)

LYNN: We have to.

ADAM: Why?

LYNN: You know why.

ADAM: *Why!!?*

(ADAM *shrinks back into the couch, overwhelmed, terrified.*)

LYNN: Do you want to get married...you want even the chance of that? *(Beat)* Do you love me? *(Beat)* Open the door.

(Now only one beat between the knocks)

(Knock)

(Knock)

(Knock)

(ADAM *pulls himself up from the couch on weak legs and crosses to the door.* LYNN *is behind him.*)

(A moment)

(ADAM *reaches out...and slowly opens the door.*)

(All lights fade except for the light spilling in from outside.)

(They both step back, staring out for a long moment.)

LYNN: Come in.

END OF PLAY

www.ingramcontent.com/pod-product-compliance
Lightning Source LLC
Chambersburg PA
CBHW052217090426
42741CB00010B/2571